The Purpose Builder

Plan. Design. Create.

by

Willie E. Mays, Jr.

Anointed To Reign Publishers Inc.

The Purpose Builder / 2

Anointed to Reign Publishing, located in the United States of America publishes this document. The information in this document is accurate and current to the best of the ability and knowledge of the author at the time of writing. The content of the document is subject to change without notice.

ISBN 10: 0-9741678-3-5

ISBN 13: 978-0-9741678-3-1

For inquiries and speaking information please contact:

Will Motivates: A division of Willie Mays Ministries
4357 Spindlewick Lane
Douglasville, GA 30135
888.718.1970
www.willmotivates.com
contact@willmotivates.com

Cover design by DaLaHe Media

The Purpose Builder

Plan. Design. Create.

By Willie E. Mays, Jr.

Table of Contents

Introduction

The Expressway to Purpose

The Building of Purpose

FOREWORD

Over the many years of Christian ministry and leadership, I've come to realize that it is not what happens *to* you in life as much as what happens *in* you in life that determines greatness and significance—this can only be discovered when knowing your purpose. Willie E. Mays, Jr. has nailed it! He has been both divinely appointed and anointed for such a time this—to critically think through and advise the many of tomorrow's generation on the importance of both finding and fulfilling one's purpose in life.

From the very onset of Mays' powerful thoughts and writings, all will clearly know and understand the master plan of success and significance—planning, designing and creating a culture of *purpose* found and *purpose* fulfilled. *The Purpose Builder* is a book that is simply riveting and provoking! It is indeed a must read for every student, entrepreneur, community leader, and clergy leader!
~ Dr. Michael A. Stevens, Sr.

Dr. Michael A. Stevens, Sr., D. Min
Author of *We Too, Stand: A Call for the African-American Church to Support the Jewish State* (Frontline Publishing, 2013). Dr. Stevens is also author of *No More Excuses: Creating a Culture in the Church to Reach African-American Men (Charisma House, 2008)* and *Straight Up: The Church's Official Response to the Epidemic of Downlow Living (Creation House, 2006).*

No Purpose = No Life

Purpose is the Key to Life

"The two most important days in your life are the day you are born and the day you find out why."
~Mark Twain

Introduction

Wouldn't it be nice if you were born knowing your purpose without any doubts? As a Purpose Builder of people, one of the biggest challenges people face today is living life not knowing their purpose. College students are so unsure of their purpose that 50% - 70% of college students change their major at least once; and most change it at least three times before they graduate. And even after they graduate college, those that go on to work in their educational field on average change careers at least seven times. According to Forbes, the "Job Hopping" is the new normal for Millennials. It's not that people are changing careers that often because they are tired, because they are bored, or because they are not making enough money. People are changing careers because they are not finding self-fulfillment in their career. As people, when we are not living in our purpose, we will find ourselves bored, frustrated, unfulfilled, and worse; without hope.

The Purpose Builder is here to help you build your purpose. The Purpose Builder is not another book about someone sharing with you about themselves and their purpose, but a book that shows you how to discover your purpose and live in that purpose. With the Purpose Builder, you will start building your purpose before you finish reading this book. You will begin to discover the purpose that was planted on the inside of you before you arrived. You will begin to find out why you are here on this earth. You will be confident of your purpose and you will be able to help others discover their purpose. You will not waste another year, another month, or another week living without your purpose. It's time to discover your purpose today!

Chapter 1

The Importance of Knowing Your Purpose

"The greatest thing in this world is not so much where we stand as in what direction we are moving."
— **Johann Wolfgang von Goethe**

One of the greatest challenges we are facing in our society now is that many people know where they are, but they have no clue where they are going. Every day, more and more people are taking time to "find themselves."

When people are in their adolescent years, it is understandable that we might hear them say that they are unsure of what they would like to do when they grow up. However, we are now seeing young adults and mature adults alike that are unsure of where they are headed in life. It is incomprehensible to hear those that are now mature adults that have no direction as to where they are headed. As it stands now, every generation seems to be losing a sense of self and purpose. During the last several generations, people had a plan to get married, have kids, create a family, and so on. Now in today's generation, people are unsure of who they are, where they want to be, and even what they want out of life. Fifty years ago, people knew they wanted to be married and have a family; it was part of their individual life purpose. That statistic has changed drastically and consequently, people are further without purpose.

At this point, you are probably thinking, "what does marriage have to do with anything"? I'm glad you asked; PLENTY! Here is what marriage says about individuals that say "I do".

Marriage says:

- I have a plan and purpose for family
- I have a plan and purpose for future with others
- I have a plan and purpose for finances
- I have a plan and purpose for living

- I have a plan and purpose to impact the lives of others

And sure, there are so many other things that marriage says, however, it says that there is some purpose in who I am. This is not to say that you don't have purpose if you are not married, however this is just an example of how purpose has been lost, abused, and distorted over the last several years.

Why is it so important to know your purpose?

Think about this, when you have no destination, every road you turn down will get you where you are going. How many times have you done a retrospective look at your life only to find that you have not advanced as much as you would have liked? How many times have you ever felt like your life wasn't making an impact to those around you; and more importantly to yourself? These types of questions come when you are not living a life of purpose. The happiness of your life is tied up in your purpose. When you are not living on purpose, you will often feel frustrated, you will sometimes feel like your life has no meaning, you have those days at work where you feel like you are in a dead-end job with no hope of doing anything greater. Purpose defies all of those previous thoughts. Purpose gives you a reason to wake up, purpose gives you a reason to live, and believe it or not, purpose gives you a reason to die. As a matter of fact, if the thing in which you are living for isn't enough to die for, then why are you living for it? You need to understand that your purpose is so much greater than your world. You were created because of purpose. You exist because there was a purpose to be filled and you are the answer to fulfilling that purpose. Everything and everybody was created for a reason and for a purpose. Most often the challenge is in knowing for what purpose we were created. Once you discover that purpose, you will unlock your potential, unlock your career, unlock your family, unlock your finances, and most importantly, unlock your destiny.

What is the Value of Purpose?

The value of purpose is different depending on who you ask. There are those that say their purpose has no value, and those that say that their purpose is priceless; both are right. The value of purpose can be summed up in three areas.

1. **People**. When you are not living a life of purpose, you have no clue of the countless lives that you are destroying or disappointing. When you mention the name Mordecai Ham, most people do not know him or recognize his name. Conversely, when you mention the name Billy Graham, he is well known and his name is recognized around the world. The reason most of us know Billy Graham is because of Mordecai Ham. Mordecai Ham was a man of purpose and living a life of purpose. Could you imagine if Mordecai Ham was not living in his purpose? Would he have

ever met the young Billy Graham during a
revival in Charlotte, North Carolina in 1934?
If Mordecai Ham would have been like those
who decide not to live a life of purpose and
had not done a revival in 1934, where would
all those hundreds of thousands of people be
that Billy Graham has touched?   How about
the name Clifton (Pop) Herring? Does that
ring a bell? No? Don't worry, you are not
alone. However, this name rings a bell to
most around the world: Michael Jordan. Yes,
Clifton (Pop) Herring was Michael Jordan's
high school basketball coach. Coach Herring
was living a life of purpose and understanding
that his purpose had value. Not just because
his purpose was instrumental in helping to
produce arguably the greatest basketball
player of all time, but also because his
purpose touched countless lives of youth to
encourage, teach, train, and inspire them to
live their purpose. And the list continues,

however the point is, part of the value of your purpose is the people your purpose will touch.

2. **Productivity**. In my own terms, productivity is the measured result of being productive. Purpose makes you productive. When you live a life on purpose, you have measurable achievements that are directly related to your purpose. Ed Zitron said in an article that he published on "Inc.com" that "when employees felt like they were working towards a good cause, it increased their productivity by 30%." If a company can see an increase in productivity simply by living a life of purpose, what can happen to your life when you start living a life of purpose? What areas would you like to see increase in your personal life? Health? Wealth? Family? Business? All of these areas plus many others can increase their productivity by simply giving them purpose.

Since purpose has measurable results, how should you measure them? There are a number of ways to measure them, but I would suggest something that is very common: S.M.A.R.T. goals. Here is how we define the acronym

Setting SMART Goals

SMART is an acronym for:

Specific: by making your goals specific, you bring clarity and focus

Measurable: helps you keep track of your progress

Attainable: keeps your goals realistic and you motivated

Relevant: keeps the focus on something you truly want to accomplish

Time-Bound: helps you set targets with deadlines

S.M.A.R.T.

S. – Specific. Be specific about what it is you are planning and pursuing. Being specific about your plans that lead to your purpose will give you a precise scope. Many people take years to discover their purpose because they have no specific plans to get there. When you are specific in your plans, you can easily check off those goals when you attain them. For example, if my plans are to "go west," what determines when I arrive? If I go 2 feet in a westerly direction, or if I go 200 miles, I still went west. However, if I plan to go west to San Diego, California (specific) I can measure my goal of making it there because I was specific.

M. – Measurable. Your purpose produces measurable results. In other words, your purpose has milestones that tell you that you are moving in your purpose. The other thing that measurable results tell you is when you have gone on a tangent and somehow gotten off track. Here is the challenge that many people face. People will start off well in their purpose, but somewhere along the way, they get diverted and never get back on track; therefore, loosing visibility of their purpose. When your purpose is measurable and you are not producing, the lack of productivity reminds you that you are off track. Remember, purpose produces measurable results. If there is nothing to measure there is no purpose being produced. One of the things that I have found to be very helpful in obtaining measured results is to add small milestones to measure on my destination to fulfilling purpose. I add things that won't take a long time to complete. Completing these thing in a timely manner gives me a sense of accomplishment and encouragement that I can continue on with those other tasks that may serve to be much more difficult. I will talk more about this under the next section: Attainable

A. Attainable. One thing that I have never liked about New Year's Resolutions is that people often times make these "un-attainable" goals. Notice I didn't say that they were impossible. Unattainable and impossible are not the same thing. Impossible says that there is no way for it to be done. Conversely, unattainable says that a person is not willing to do what it takes to attain the goal that has been set.

R. Relevant. You must keep your goals and focus on something you wish to accomplish. One of the things that so many people fall prey to is that they often times try to choose goals that are not marked particularly by things that they want to accomplish. If you are going to set goals for life based on money, be sure to find things that you really want to accomplish. So many people adventure off to do things that they don't necessarily interest them, but the career path might be financially rewarding. After going through several years to obtain a certain salary, only to find out after being honest with themselves that what they are doing is not anything that they really wanted to do. According to www.careers-advice-online.com, the average person will change careers 5-7 times in their lifetime. This is not something that is driven by money; completely. There are times when a person decides that they want "an upgrade" in lifestyle and decide that they want a career change. However, in most cases, people change because they are not keeping their goals relevant. Keep your goals relevant to you and you will continue to peruse after them. The moment they lose relevancy, your drive and determination to pursue diminishes.

T. Time-Bound. Effective goals have deadlines. We as people learn goals and deadlines while growing up. We play(ed) video games that have goals and deadlines such as sports games with periods, quarters, and halves. We learned goals and deadlines while in school taking standardized tests. During grade school, every few years there would be a standardized test. Before you would start a certain section of the test, they would tell you something like, "you have 25 minutes to complete this portion of the test." Going into college, there were standardized tests such as the ACT and SAT. These tests are geared not only to test your academia, but they are also geared at testing how well you deal with goals and deadlines. And then when you go into the workforce, there are goals and deadlines on every level. So, the point is, for all of our lives, we have been learning that there are goals and deadlines in everything we do. How is it that we spend a lifetime learning this but at the same time we can do such a poor job setting goals and deadlines with our life and purpose? One of the best feelings of satisfaction is to be able to set a goal for a deadline and you accomplish the goal by the deadline. The deadline is not set to fail you, but it has been set to keep you on track for the greater purpose. Set and keep those deadlines!

Chapter 2

How Do I Discover My Purpose?

"What am I living for and what am I dying for are the
same question."
— **Margaret Atwood**

As a leader of people, one of the questions that I
get asked often, "how do I know what my purpose is?"
(if only I had $1.00 for every time I was asked that
question.) The fascinating, and yet adventurous thing
about purpose is that purpose has to be discovered.
You can't choose as an individual what you want your
purpose to be, but you need to understand that you
exist because of your purpose. Because God is such
a purposeful God, He created you because there was
a purpose to be fulfilled. There is nobody created that
God didn't create without a purpose. They way this
process works is like this. Imagine if you will, God has
a bucket of balls. Each ball is a purpose. So
essentially, God has a bucket of purpose. And what

God does is He creates people to help fulfill the
purpose that already exists outside of time, here on
earth. That is why I know that there are no such
things as people being born as an accident. Because
the only reason why God created them is because He
already had a purpose to be fulfilled.

As I mentioned to you earlier in this chapter, many
people have come my way to ask me the question
about how they discover their purpose? That answer
is much easier said than done. The answer is simple.
In the bible, Jesus shows us the key to discovering
our purpose. The way that the Apostles and Disciples
discovered their purpose was by helping Jesus fulfill
His purpose. Do you get this very simple principle
being displayed? One of the best and fastest ways to
discover your purpose is to help someone else
discover their purpose. The challenge is that many
people are unwilling to help other discover their
purpose for various reasons. We live lives that are
super busy and the world is at our fingertips.
Discovering your purpose may cost you some

sacrifice in order to discover it. You may not discover your purpose overnight. Notice that the disciples literally dropped what they were doing and started life new following Jesus. They wanted Jesus to win in purpose so desperately that all of them discovered their purpose. Now this text is in no way indicating that you need to drop everything that you are doing to go help someone discover their purpose, however it is saying that if you are tired of living your life every day without the satisfaction of walking in your purpose, you are going to have to sacrifice some things.

Choosing the person to help discover purpose

You should be very selective of who you choose to help discover purpose with. Remember, you are talking about someone now that has influence and impact on your future. You are talking about someone you are trusting with your future development. When you choose someone to help discover your purpose, try to choose someone that is already operating in their purpose. Don't just pick your friend because you've been friends for 20 years. While your friend

John might be a great guy, if John is not moving and living on purpose and has no desires to live a life of purpose, then John is not the one. Remember, we don't choose friends based on purpose, we choose them based on character. They may have great character, but no definite purpose.

The person(s) that you choose to help discover your purpose should be someone that has already proven that they are living their own life on purpose. That means that they have a plan set that they are following. They can show you their plan and you can physically look at their plan and see where they are in their plan. Why was Jesus so successful as showing others how to live a life on purpose? Glad you asked. Jesus followed a written plan that was his purpose. His plan could be followed by him and others. The reason why many people knew who he was even without meeting him and never seeing him before is because when they say him, he matched the plan that he had already shown them about who he was and what he was doing. Whoever you follow may not have a plan that they are following like Jesus, but they do have a plan that is being followed.

Not only do you choose people that are following a plan, but try to choose someone that is following a plan like the plan that you would want to have set for your own life. There might be a local mechanic in the area who is living a very good life on purpose. He may have a plan that you can easily see that he is following. While that mechanic may be a good person for someone to follow to discover purpose; if you have plans to be a doctor, that mechanic is probably not your best option. You need to make the sacrifice to find and be present to those that you are looking to learn from. The student sacrifices to be with the teacher, not the other way around. As an individual, you need to identify a few people that can deposit into your life, and they have nothing to gain from you, and nothing to lose if you were no longer a part of their life. Those are the individuals that can speak truth freely to you and tell you what you need to hear, not just what you want to hear. You need people in your life that will challenge you to get to your purpose. You need people in your life who are doing better than you are; that can help pull you up when you are down. If you are at the top of the circle in your circle of friends, at some point you will find that everyone around you is pulling you down and there is nobody around to help pull you up. If you are at the top of the circle, you need to turn the circle and allow some others to come in to your circle, as well as find some other circles to join.

Chapter 3

Know Your Destination

In Stephen Covey's book, "The 7 Habits of Highly Effective People" habit 2 says, "Begin with The End in Mind." In order to have a good definiteness of purpose, you need to know where you are going even before you get started. One of the many challenges of life is figuring out the destination that you want to have in life. Many people spend years traveling around the expressways of life with no destination. Have you ever noticed people that seem to be going in circles? Spending years of their life working hard but never progressing? What is the use of working hard year after year to go further in life, but keep ending up in the same place? This is a result of driving down the expressway with no destination. A wise man once told me, "when you know the what, the how becomes much easier." Most of us know that in order to move, we must put action to work, however many of us are have either neutral or negative action. When a person is moving without a destination, that is a neutral action. It is not moving you to your purpose, but it is not moving you away from your purpose either. A negative action or movement are when you make moves that have the potential to hold you back from getting to your purpose. For example, going to jail doesn't have to stop you from getting to your purpose, but it does and can have a negative effect on your reaching your purpose. That is why it is important to know where you are going before you get started. Knowing where you are going before you get started also gives you your boundaries of what you can and can't do. It will tell you what you need in order to make your destination. If my destination is to make it to Hawaii from Georgia, I know from knowledge (maps, Google, etc.) that it will take more than a car to get there. So, my purpose tells me that in order to get there, I need some alternate modes of transportation to get me where I need to be.   Your destination tells you all the resources, tools, training, etc. that it will take to get where you are going. Many times, we have a destination in mind but we are no willing to do the work involved to get where we need to be. We have a destination purpose to be a Doctor, but we don't want to spend time in undergrad and medical school to get us there. We know that we want to be a lawyer, but we don't want to sacrifice and go to law school. If you are not willing to do what it takes to get to where you want to go, you really don't want to get to that destination.

If I had a choice in what classes were offered in school that would really help in life, one of those classes would be called, "Destination". Can you imagine the impact that we would have on our youth and young adults growing up if we were able to help them identify their destinations early in life? How much time could you have saved if only you knew what you wanted to be before you went to college? How much time would you have saved if only you knew that instead of going to college, you were "cut out" for military? Or being a business owner? See, my point is this, we spend so much time trying to pinpoint the destination that we don't leave travel time to get to the destination. Although people are wired very different in their thought process, one thing is certain in all of us; we all have a destination that we are trying to get to. Some of us are driving fast to get there, some are on cruise control, and then there are those that have literally parked the car and just taking time to explore where they are. None are any more or less important than the other, but at least they know the destination that they are going.

A personal pet peeve of mine is when I leave a place without having a plan for where I am going before I leave. (Notice I said have a plan BEFORE I leave.) I personally am one who likes to know all of the stops I am going to make and in what order I plan to make them. On that same token, I am the same way when I go into a shopping center. I like to know what shopping center I am going to and what store(s) I am planning to go to at that shopping center before I get there. For me, I don't like to have to go in and out of the same stores multiple times in the same trip, or have to create zig zags going from store to store. When I do that, I feel like I am somehow going backwards in life. Such is the way with our destination. You want to have a clear plan and outline of where you are going and how you plan to get there. You know the old adage, "if you fail to plan, you plan to fail." All of us at some time in our life have failed to plan, and we saw the results of that. Sometimes it worked out, but most of the time, we are very inefficient because we tried it without a plan.

I can recall growing up, my family took lots of family vacations. When I say family, I am not only talking my immediate family, but I am talking extended family. Aunts, Uncles, Cousins, etc. So, there would literally be 40-50 or more of us on a vacation together. On one of these particular vacations, we traveled from Michigan to Washington D.C. For those of you familiar with Washington D.C., traffic can be a monster; and worse at certain times of the day. So as fate, and D.C. traffic would have it, our family has a multiple car motorcade traveling around the beltway known as I-495. And after plenty of intense conversation between the "family chiefs" about what was the right way to go, we finally started moving. The family tribe was finally in cheer after we had been sitting on the side of the expressway in the middle of rush hour traffic for over an hour. After traveling by motorcade for nearly 3 hours, someone finally notices an object on the side of the expressway that looks familiar. It looked familiar because it was familiar. After traveling for over 3 hours, only to find that we had only traveled 2 MILES! At that moment the wind had been let out of everybody's sail. Our feelings of hope and conquer had been replaced with despair and desperation. After spending the whole day on I-495, we all realized that we could have avoided all of that headache if only we would have had the right plan.

Quick brain homework: Think about a time when you operated without a plan. How did it go? Was it a successful mission? If you would have made a plan, would that mission have turned out better? Would it have cost you less time? Would it have cost you less money? Think about some things that you have on your plate that needs to get done. Make a plan on how you will get it done and then ask yourself if you feel efficient in how you done it.

Chapter 4

Know Your Vehicle

I can remember purchasing a vehicle once before and looking for the owner's manual. When I looked in the glove compartment where the owner's manual is usually located, I didn't see it. So, I went into the dealership to ask for it and they told me that customers have to request it. I can remember asking the salesman why isn't it placed in the vehicle automatically. He responded that most people don't use them so they don't put them in the vehicle unless requested. As I thought about what had just taken place, the question that I asked myself is, "how does the owner of the vehicle know the capabilities of the vehicle without the manual?" The challenge that many people face with their vehicle is that they get vehicles based on things such as looks, popularity, and what they think the vehicle is capable of. While the vehicle might be capable of the things that we think that it is able to do, how many other capabilities does the vehicle offer that we are not using because we have not read the owner's manual?

Why is it so important to "know your car" on the destination to purpose? Glad you asked. Knowing the capabilities of your car is one of the variables that determine how long it takes before you get to your purpose. Without knowing the capabilities of your car, you really don't know if the car you are driving is even capable of getting you to your purpose or not. What do I mean by all of this jargon talking about a car and capabilities as it relates to purpose? Case in point: I remember when I was in high school several years ago, I knew then I wanted to be an Electrical Engineer. However, my counselor had me in courses that would lead to becoming a teacher. While there is nothing wrong with becoming a teacher, it just wasn't the "vehicle" that was going to get me to where I was trying to go. Not only is it important to know the capabilities of the vehicle to get us where we are going, but it can be very helpful to know someone else that has some experience with the type of vehicle that you need. In common terms we call this person a "mentor." One of the many challenges that I had was that I knew that I wanted to be an Engineer, but I had no clue on the type of courses I needed in high school to become an Engineer. Unbeknownst to me, I found out later that my counselor didn't know what classes I needed to become an Engineer either. As a result, when I got to college, I found out that I was taking classes that I didn't need and classes I needed, I didn't take. So, my Freshmen year of college was all about playing catch up. Other Freshmen in college that were there to study engineering were so much further ahead than I was. I had to work twice as hard to try to play catch up. This scenario would have been totally different had I known someone else that had "driven the same car" as I was attempting to drive. Again, so many times we have a destination in mind, but have no clue on how to get there. Part of the reason that so many people don't make their destination is because they had no clue what would be included on the journey to their destination. Often times people find out that there are things along the journey that they are not willing to go through, and therefore forfeit their destination. It's always interesting to me the route that the GPS gives when you allow it to give you direction. I find that many times, the GPS is not so much concerned about what you have to go through to get to your destination as it is making sure that you took the most direct route. Sometimes, the most direct route is not the most desirable route. There are those that are willing to take the less desirable route to make it to their destination faster; and then there are those that would prefer to take the longer, yet scenic route to get to their destination. The GPS understands well that its purpose is to get you to your destination in the fastest manner.

If you have others involved in your life such as a spouse and/or child you will need to consider them when considering your destination. Does your destination include them? Will they be a part of your journey to your destination? How much support will you need from them during the journey to make your destination? These are all important questions to ask yourself while attaining your purpose. While it is "your" purpose, those in your life that are connected to you have a great deal of influence on you attaining your purpose. How much will their lives be impacted by your purpose? While on the road to your purpose, are you OK with having to make some detours and pit stops along the way to give attention to those that are in the vehicle with you? Remember, the vehicle you choose on the road to purpose is a very integral part to making it to your destination.

Chapter 5

Determine Your Lane

Living in Metro Atlanta, I have found that there is no way to escape being in traffic. As a matter of fact, in a 2008 study done by Forbes, they ranked Atlanta #1 out of the 75 biggest cities in America as having the worst traffic in the United States. (Magazine, 2008) Since traffic is such a daily part of many people's life; especially here in Atlanta, it is important to determine your lane of travel. By design, the slower lanes on the expressway are generally to the right and the faster lanes are to the left. In some places, the expressway consists of two lanes, and in other places, it consists of multiple lanes. One of the things that I love about traveling on the expressways in Atlanta is that you have the option of choosing what lane you want to travel to your destination in. The reason this is important is because when you are traveling behind someone in a lane, you are limited to traveling at the speed that they travel at in front of you. If you are on a one lane road and the car in front of you is going 35mph, you have no choice in going faster than 35mph. It is possible that the driver of the vehicle in front of you may think that they are going fast already. Maybe they are going fast enough for themselves, but they may not be going the speed that you need to go. However, when you are on an eight-lane expressway, if someone is not going the speed that you want to be able to go, you have the option of choosing a different lane and going around them. You are not limited to going the speed that the driver in front of you is driving. Without regard to traffic, how fast you get to your destination is totally dependent upon you. Such is life! When you are traveling the expressway of life to get to your purpose, you want to choose to be on the expressway with multiple lanes, not just one. When you need to speed up, you need to have the option to move around those that may be holding you back. You need to be able to identify those that are traveling with you and slowing you down and those that are fueling your progress. Here is an easy way to figure out the difference between the two. If a person is not doing much to get to their own destination and figure out their own purpose, they will not be in a hurry to help you get to yours.

Chapter 6

Determine Your Speed

"There are no speed limits on the road to success." -

David W. Johnson

Speed is all about how fast you want to get
something done. Speed is our measurement to our
desired, or undesired, results. We even measure
where we travel based on speed. We want to know
the answer to the age old famous question, "Are we
there yet? How much longer?" These questions
among others are determined by how fast you are
going. If you have a destination in mind and you know
how far it is away, you can determine how long it will
take you to get there based on how fast you drive.
Ironically, sometimes driving may not get you there
fast enough, so then you might decide to take a plane,
helicopter, or a jet. These are all modes of

transportation to get you to a desired destination in a certain amount of time. When it comes to purpose, the speed you drive determines how long it will take you to get to your purpose. Speed determines, if you will even make it to your destination. When it comes to purpose speed is equivalent to motivation. Those that have little to no motivation often take much longer to get to their destination than those with an abundance of motivation. Motivation says how bad you want or desire a thing. Motivation can come in different forms, but it does the same thing. It pushes you to a purpose. You have to decide what your motivation is going to be. Whatever your motivation is, make sure that it is strong enough to keep you going even when you want to give up. The challenge that many people have is that their motivation to succeed sometimes dwindles in the midst of their pursuit of purpose. How many times have you or someone you know made a New Year's resolution that lasted less than three months? Less than one month? Less than two weeks? It's simply because their reason(s) for going to the gym did not have a strong enough motivation tied to it. The stronger the motivation, the faster your speed to your purpose will be. Using the same example above with the person starting a New Year's resolution and going to the gym; lets change the scenario. Instead of just making a New Year's resolution, what if the Doctor told them if they did not lose weight in the next year they would die? There is a much stronger motivation tied to the goal now. Now my motivation is a must. When your motivation is strong enough, you will increase your speed to your purpose and guarantee yourself to make your destination.

There is a lot to be learned from living in a metropolis. Atlanta, Ga is the metropolis of the Southeast United States. The metro Atlanta expressway system is one of the most frustrating things about living in Atlanta. Most expressways are set up so that the right lane is the slow lane and the further you move lanes to the left, those are considered the fast or passing lanes. In Atlanta, every lane can be used as a passing lane. If the person in front of you is not going fast enough, you can choose ANY open lane to pass the vehicle in front of you. In life, you have to decide that the speed in which you make it to your destination will not be controlled by someone else. If you take years to get there, or worse, never get there at all, nobody else is going to take responsibility for it. Since you have to take responsibility for your own actions, you need to control the speed towards your purpose. Don't allow anyone else to stand in the way of you and your purpose.

Never confuse someone clearing the way to your purpose for someone standing in the way of your purpose. What's the difference? I'm glad you asked. There will be times when you need someone to help clear the way to your purpose. Imagine a pregnant mother on the way to the hospital and her water breaks on the way. She calls the police and they give a police escort to make it to their destination quicker. This is someone clearing the way to purpose. This is when someone who is specially trained to get unnecessary distractions out of your way so that you can make it to your purpose safely and without distractions. They may or may not be with you when you start, but they will be there to see you through to your purpose. And they will not want anything in return as it is their purpose to help get you to your purpose.

The Building of Purpose

Chapter 7

3 Tiers to Purpose

1. Discovery
2. Apprenticeship
3. Mentorship

1. Discovery of Purpose

I quoted early in this book a famous saying by
Mark Twain that one of the two most
important days in your life is the day that you
discover your purpose. Unfortunately, there
are a lot of people who are born and never
discover their purpose. What is worse is that
they never seek to discover their purpose.
Can you imagine the tragedy of life to be born

with purpose and never seek to discover what it is? That is like being born with a gift of $1,000,000.00 that is attached to your name; and all you have to do is discover where it is. Who wouldn't spend time searching for the $1,000,000.00 that already belongs to them? I know I would!

Discovery of your purpose is the most important step in the 3 Tiers to Purpose. If you never discover your purpose, the last two tiers become irrelevant. With this being said, you may now be asking, "how do I discover my purpose?" Great, I thought you would never ask. To discover your purpose, you need to open your heart and be sensitive to what your heart, mind, and soul is telling you and leading you to. You need to take a face value that God is an amazing God! God has caused us to gravitate towards our purpose. There is a magnetic force in us that causes us to gravitate towards our purpose. Have you

ever noticed that there are some things that
you just do well without even practicing?
Often times it will seem like there is no way
"that" can be your purpose because it is too
easy. Many times, we think that our purpose
has to be something massive and super
complex. Everyone is not called to be a
Rocket Scientist and neither is everyone
called to be a Physicist. Some of us are
called to the complex things in life, and some
are called to the simple things in life. Don't
discredit yourself no matter what you are
called to. While I am not old by any means at
the time of writing this book, I have been
around the block a few times. I used to think
that I wanted to be this whiz kid that lived in
New York City and had the answer to at least
one of the world's problems. The older, and
wiser I might add, that I got, I realized that
solving the simple things in life gave me great
joy. I realized that more people were dealing

with simple things that complex things. Very few people are dealing with complex things, but everybody has some everyday simple challenges taking place every day. So, I begin to focus on the simple challenges of life. In doing so, I found my purpose. My point to you is that as you wake up every day, examine what your heart is leading you towards. The thing(s) that you keep gravitating back to can be, and most likely is your purpose.

2. Apprenticeship of Purpose

This very important step of purpose is often overlooked and undervalued. It seems these days that nobody wants to be in the very important role of an apprentice anymore. Some of the greatest people that we have ever witnessed in our lifetime and before were all an apprentice of someone. Here are a few examples of this very important relationship.

Maya Angelou mentored Oprah Winfrey;
former Apple CEO, the late Steve Jobs,
mentored Facebook CEO Mark Zuckerberg;
Dr. Benjamin Mays was mentor to Dr. Martin
Luther King Jr.; Father Michael van mentored
Mother Teresa der Peet; Christian Dior
mentored Yves St. Laurent; and Warren
Buffett mentored Bill Gates. The list goes on,
my point is that greatness produces
greatness. I'm not saying that greatness
cannot come of its own, however there is a
solid history with greater achievement when a
person is an apprentice. With this being said,
why don't more people take advantage of this
role? Some consider being an apprentice as
being a flunky. Some simply don't want to
serve. Some people feel like it is beneath
them to serve someone else. Even Jesus
who was the greatest to ever walk this earth
said that he came here on earth to serve. I
believe that Jesus served to show all of us

something valuable. Think about it, why would Jesus have to serve anybody? He is the king of this world. I believe that Jesus served to show us that the best, and most solid way to move up was through serving. Even Jesus knew that he couldn't be exalted to his father unless he served first. As you can see from the list above, being an apprentice and serving as a mentee develops your roots for growth. After you discover your purpose, find yourself a mentor to serve and grown under.

3. Mentorship of Purpose

To complete purpose, it is important to understand that our purpose is not meant to die off with us when we die. Our purpose was created before us and it is intended to live on after us. In order for this to happen, we have to open ourselves us to be Mentors. We have to allow our purpose to be passed on to others without fear of loss. We need to remember that our purpose doesn't belong to us anyway, it belongs to the one that gave it to us. I know that it is easy to get possessive of purpose. You pour so much of yourself into your purpose. Your pour your time, your talents, and your treasure into your purpose and consequently you feel like it belongs to you. Even after pouring all of yourself in to your purpose, it still doesn't belong to you. You have to remember that you were created for the purpose; the purpose wasn't created for you. And guess what, there are others that were created to carry out the purpose that you are now helping to fulfill. So, it is important to take what you have and pass it on to the next generation so that purpose lives on.

Do you have any family or friends that have passed on who were great cooks? How many of them took time to write out recipes and teach you their secrets of cooking? So many times, we have Grandmothers, Aunties, and Uncles who were great cooks and had great recipes and they passed on taking those recipes to the grave with them. Can you imagine if you had just half of your Grandma's recipes? You could open up one of the greatest restaurants on this side of heaven. Don't let this be your purpose. Don't take your purpose to the grave with you. Leave yourself open to be a mentor to someone else that has gravitated to your purpose. It just may be that they have discovered their purpose by watching you.

Chapter 8

Purpose Reflections

Purpose Reflections

Miriam-Webster defines reflection as the production of an image by or as if by a mirror, or an effect produced by an influence.

For this chapter, I would like to focus on the second part of the definition, "an effect produced by an influence." As I told you many times throughout this book, purpose is discovered. Purpose is often discovered by its gravitational pull to itself. In other words, when we see others living the purpose which we have, there is a gravitational pull towards it. Part of the challenge we have in today's society is that we have fewer and fewer people living on purpose. The generational reflection effect is that when our younger generation is trying to discover their purpose, it is becoming harder for them to find. When they are looking at the generation ahead of them for purpose reflection, they are finding fewer people walking in their purpose. Consequently, they don't find their purpose because the reflections that they are looking at are not living in their purpose. The next generation is becoming what is being reflected; a generation with no purpose. Have you ever wondered how so many in this millennial generation can sit for hours and play video games or they can turn 30 or 35 and still live at home with their parents and don't feel a need to leave the nest? It's simple: they are doing what they see reflected. That wasn't the generation X. The generation X had a reflection of the "Baby Boomers". What the Baby Boomers reflected to us was work ethic and responsibility. They taught us the value of work and independence. GenX'ers were eager to get out of the nest and fly independently. GenX'ers were ready to spread their wings and fly along; even if they were not really ready to fly alone, they were willing to try.

This is because of what was reflected to them by the Baby Boomers. If we are ever going to see people start living in their purpose again, we have to give them something to look at. How do you do this? Give them something to reflect on. Even if you are unsure of your purpose, be so busy trying to discover your purpose that at least you pass on the trait on being busy trying to discover your purpose. One thing is for sure; your purpose is not hiding from you. If you are seeking it, eventually you will find it.

> Every day, ask yourself the question, "What did I leave for the next generation of Purpose Seekers to reflect on? If your answer is nothing, that is exactly what they are going to see when they look at your reflection: nothing!

Chapter 9

Purpose Connections

The old saying says, "birds of a feather flock together." There is certainly something to be said about that saying. It is evident that you don't have to match up birds of a feather; they eventually come together. A wise person once told me if you want to know how people see you, look at your five closest friends. With purpose, just as in life, it is important to get around those that embrace your purpose. People will either embrace or disgrace your purpose. If they are not embracing your purpose, somewhere they are disgracing your purpose. They may not try to disgrace your purpose intentionally, but at some point, they will if they haven't yet. You want to get around people that believe in you and your purpose. You want to be around those that will encourage and uplift you in your purpose. You want to be around those that will not let you give up on your purpose when it gets tough and you want to throw in the towel. If someone lets you attempt to throw in the towel every time your purpose gets rough, they are not embracing your purpose, but rather they are disgracing it. What they are saying is that they don't believe in you and your purpose. Michael Jordan had to practice hours upon hours in high school just to make the team. I'm sure there were countless times that he wanted to throw in the towel, however his father wouldn't allow him to throw in the towel. His father believed in his purpose and wouldn't allow Michael to give up on his purpose. Can you imagine if young Michael Jordan would have given up on his purpose? What a gift the rest of this world would have missed. Oprah Winfrey often talks about the adversity and racism she went through starting off as a news Anchor in Tennessee. Can you imagine what would have happened if Maya Angelou would have allowed young Oprah to give up on her purpose? Would we have ever seen the Oprah

Winfrey Show? Would we have ever seen OWN Network? Would we have ever known Dr. Phil, or Rachel Ray? My point is that you have to have some true Purpose Connections in your life. Purpose Connections are people that help to connect you to your purpose. Who are your Purpose Connections in life? Do you have any? At least one? If not, you need to find one fast. Your purpose is depending on your Purpose Connection.

Chapter 10

Living on Purpose

Section 1: No Purpose = No Life
Section 2: Purpose is the Key to Life

Section 1: No Purpose = No Life

We understand from our research and reading that we were created to fill purpose. Since we were created to fill purpose, it can be concluded that if we are not living for purpose, we are not living; we are just merely existing. There is a very bold difference with living versus existing. Just because you are breathing and here on earth doesn't equate to living. There are people right now who are in a vegetative state of being. They are here because of a breathing tube, no brain function, no movement of the body, but yet they are here. This is not to say that they won't function again, but as of now, they are existing. As a matter of fact, there are many people that have made the request that if they are ever in that state of "existing" to pull the life chord and allow them to die. Very few people want to just exist. So, since you have the opportunity, why not start living today. I don't care about how much time you have wasted; how much time has passed. I'm more interested in the time that you have in front of you to make a difference in your life and those that are waiting on you to live in your purpose. The nice thing about purpose is that it is ready whenever you get ready. Which brings me to the next section:

Section 2: Purpose is the Key to Life

When I say that purpose is the key to life, it is the key to living. You will find that when you start living a life of purpose, all of a sudden you give your life an upgrade. You give your life meaning. Purpose gives you a reason to wake up in the morning. Purpose will give you a reason to plan for the future. Many people don't plan for the future because they don't see a need for it. Purpose gives you a need to plan for the future because your purpose has a plan on being here tomorrow, next week, next month, next year, and even when you are gone. Don't let life get by you and you never take the opportunity to live. Start living today by Building Your Purpose! I am the Purpose Builder!

The Purpose Builder

Plan. Design. Create.

Acknowledgments

To my parents, Willie & Terri Mays Sr who have always believed in me and supported me; your faithful support is unwavering. To my #1 Fan and motivator, my wife Chiquita Mays, your tenacity and drive is such an inspiration. You always encourage me to take the next step. I thank God for placing me in your path over 21 years ago. To my daughters, Ja'el, Jai'dyn, Alexa, and Aliyah, you ladies have given me the greatest joy in the world to be your Daddy. The four of you are certain to be great kingdom leaders. To my Mom-in-Love, Jeanette Purifoy who had more space in her heart to take another son, thank you for your love and support. I love you all!

www.ingramcontent.com/pod-product-compliance
Lightning Source LLC
Chambersburg PA
CBHW071637040426
42452CB00009B/1666